I0759345

We Can Vote

Ann Bonwill

Content Consultant

Elizabeth Case DeSantis, M.A. Elementary Education
Julia A. Stark Elementary School, Stamford, Connecticut

Reading Consultant

Jeanne M. Clidas, Ph.D.
Reading Specialist

Children's Press®
An Imprint of Scholastic Inc.

Library of Congress Cataloging-in-Publication Data

Names: Bonwill, Ann, author.
Title: We can vote/by Ann Bonwill.
Description: New York, NY: Children's Press, an imprint of Scholastic Inc., [2019] | Series: Rookie read-about civics | Includes index.
Identifiers: LCCN 2018030274| ISBN 9780531129142 (library binding) |
ISBN 9780531137727 (pbk.)
Subjects: LCSH: Voting—United States—Juvenile literature. | Elections—United States—Juvenile literature. | Citizenship—United States—Juvenile literature. | Civics—Juvenile literature.
Classification: LCC JK1978 .B64 2019 | DDC 324.60973—dc23

Produced by Spooky Cheetah Press
Design: Keith Plechaty/kwpCreative
Creative Direction: Judith E. Christ for Scholastic Inc.

Published in 2019 by Children's Press, an imprint of Scholastic Inc.

Printed in North Mankato, MN, USA   113

1 2 3 4 5 6 7 8 9 10 R 28 27 26 25 24 23 22 21 20 19

Scholastic, Inc., 557 Broadway, New York, NY 10012.

Photographs ©: cover: Ken Karp Photography; cover background flag: phloxii/Shutterstock; cover flag bunting: LiveStock/Shutterstock; 3: Ken Karp Photography; 4: Ken Karp Photography; 7: FatCamera/iStockphoto; 9: Ken Karp Photography; 11: Ken Karp Photography; 12: Ken Karp Photography; 15: FatCamera/Getty Images; 16: Rocky89/iStockphoto; 19: fstop123/Getty Images; 20: Dennis Mosner; 23: Dennis Mosner; 25: Dennis Mosner; 25 inset voting sticker: Shotgun/Shutterstock; 27: Dennis Mosner; 28-29: Bettmann/Getty Images; 30 background notebook: HiSunnySky/Shutterstock; 30 bottom right: Ken Karp Photography; 31 top right: Ken Karp Photography; 31 center right candidate: Steve Debenport/iStockphoto; 31 center right voting booth: Dennis Mosner; 31 bottom right: Ken Karp Photography.

Table of Contents

CHAPTER 1

Our Class Votes

Our class is selecting a class pet. We can have a goldfish or a hermit crab. How will we choose? We will take a vote!

Have you ever voted in your classroom?

We look at books about goldfish and hermit crabs. We learn how to take care of them. We share what we like and don't like about each choice. Now we are ready to vote.

 Why do we read about and discuss each choice?

Everyone gets a **ballot**. We color the picture of the pet we want for our class. Next we take turns putting our ballots in the ballot box. We don't have to tell anyone which pet we voted for.

 How else might you vote on something?

Our teacher **tallies** the votes.
More kids voted for the goldfish.
That will be our class pet!

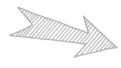 How do you feel when your choice wins?

How do you feel when your choice loses?

Goldfish

|||

CHAPTER 2

We Keep Voting

Voting is a fair way for a group to make a choice. You could vote with your friends about what game to play or what movie to watch.

 What else can you vote on?

You might also vote with your family. You could decide where to go on vacation or what to have for dinner. You could decide what to name your new family pet.

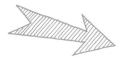 Does your little brother's vote count as much as your big sister's?

CHAPTER 3

Our Country Votes

Adults vote, too. In the United States, adults vote to choose leaders such as the mayor, the governor, and the president. People vote for leaders in a process called an election.

 Do you know who is the mayor of your town or city?

We hold a presidential election every four years. Grownups vote for the **candidate** they think will do the best job. We vote in November, and the president starts working in January.

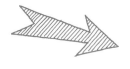 Who is the president of the United States?

Voting Today

Voting A-K

Voti

Politics

Meet the Candidates

CHAPTER 4

My Mom Votes

An election is happening soon.
My mom reads about the candidates.
She listens to them talk on television.
She learns about how the candidates
plan to help the country.

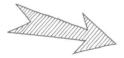 How do you learn
about things that are
important to you?

On voting day, we go to the **polls**. Our polling place is at my school. My mom goes into a voting booth. Inside the booth, she uses a computer or marks her choice on a paper ballot. People can mail their ballots if they are living far away.

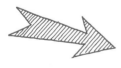 Have you ever been inside a voting booth?

My mom's vote is a secret. She does not need to tell anyone which candidate she voted for. When my mom is done, she gets a sticker to show that she voted.

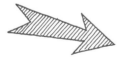 Should you ask someone which candidate they voted for?

At home we watch television to see who is winning. My mom also looks at updates on her phone. When I wake up, we will know who was elected president. I'm proud that my mom did her part. Every vote counts!

 Why is it important to vote?

Women Win

About a hundred years ago, women in the United States were not allowed to vote. People in the women's suffrage movement fought to change that law.

Men, women, and children all got involved. Girl Scouts even babysat at polling places so moms with small children could vote.

In 1920, American women finally won full voting rights.

In 1920, people everywhere celebrated women's right to vote.

the Vote ☑

Get Ready to Vote!

Here's a checklist of things to do when you vote:

- ☑ Learn as much as you can about the choices.

- ☑ Make your decision.

- ☑ Turn in your ballot.

- ☑ Find out the results.

- ☑ Be a good sport! If your side wins, remember to show respect for others when you celebrate. If your side loses, don't be a sore loser! Just try again next time.

ballot (bal-uht): a ticket, sheet of paper, or machine used to cast a secret vote
▶ *When we vote, we mark our selection on a **ballot**.*

candidate (kan-di-date): a person who is applying for a job or running in an election
▶ *People vote for their favorite* **candidate**.

polls (pohls): the place where votes are cast and recorded during an election
▶ *Adults go to the* **polls** *to vote.*

tallies (tal-eez): adds up an account, record, or score
▶ *Our teacher* **tallies** *our votes for class pet.*

Index

Facts for Now

Visit this Scholastic website for more information on voting:
www.factsfornow.scholastic.com
Enter the keyword **Vote**

About the Author

Ann Bonwill enjoys writing books for children. She has voted in every major election since she turned 18.